AF241389

THE INFLUENCE OF CONFIDENCE, DISCIPLINE & RESPECT IN LEADERSHIP

THE INFLUENCE OF
CONFIDENCE
DISCIPLINE
&
RESPECT IN
LEADERSHIP

TIMELESS PRINCIPLES TO LEAD WITH PURPOSE & INTENTION IN A MODERN WORLD

STEPHEN MILLER

This book is dedicated to those who choose to lead—not by title, but by example.

To the martial artists who step onto the training floor each day with humility, discipline, and the desire to grow. You understand that genuine strength is not simply physical, it is built through character, consistency, and respect.

To the leaders in business and in life who carry the responsibility of directing others. You make difficult decisions, stand firm in times of uncertainty, and continue forward although the path is unclear. Your devotion to excellence does not go unnoticed.

To the students who are still discovering their confidence, building their discipline, and learning the value of respect—this journey acts for you. Every great leader was formerly a novice who refused to give up.

To my Robin, whose support, patience, and belief have been the foundation of everything I have accomplished. Your presence in my life gives my work purpose and my leadership meaning.

And to those who came before me—my teachers, mentors, and role models—your lessons live on through every word written in these pages. Your influence keeps shaping not only who I am, but who I strive to become.

This book is also dedicated to the next generation of leaders.
May you guide with confidence.
May you live with discipline.
May you treat others with respect.
Let your leadership leave an impact that inspires others to do the same.

CONTENTS

THE INFLUENCE OF CONFIDENCE, DISCIPLINE & RESPECT IN LEADERSHIP

FOREWORD

It is both an honor and a privilege to write the foreword for this powerful and timely work by Grandmaster Stephen Miller—a martial artist, leader, and strategist whose influence extends far beyond the dojang and into the very fabric of leadership, business, and personal development.

In my lifetime of over four decades in martial arts training, education, and leadership development, I have come to recognize a simple but profound truth: true leadership is forged, not given. It is cultivated through discipline, sharpened through adversity, and sustained through unwavering commitment to growth and service. Grandmaster Stephen Miller embodies this truth.

The Influence of Confidence, Discipline, & Respect in Leadership is not merely a collection of ideas—*it is a blueprint*. In it, Grandmaster Miller writes from a place of lived experience. His voice reflects the mindset of a warrior and the precision of a business strategist. What makes his perspective so valuable is his ability to bridge two worlds that are often treated separately: the structured discipline of martial arts and the dynamic demands of modern leadership and business. In this work, he masterfully demonstrates that the principles of martial arts are not confined to physical training—they are, in fact, the foundation for excellence in every area of life.

Throughout these pages, you will discover that leadership is not about position or title, it is about influence, consistency, and character. Grandmaster Miller reinforces what I have taught and lived by for years: **confidence, discipline, and respect are not optional traits—they are essential pillars of effective leadership**.

What sets this book apart is its clarity of purpose. It challenges the reader to go beyond theory and into execution. It does not simply inspire it to instruct. It does not merely motivate—it equips.

As you read, you will find lessons that apply whether you are:
- A martial artist seeking to elevate your practice and leadership within your school
- A business owner striving to build systems that produce results
- A leader committed to developing people and creating lasting impact
- Or an individual on a journey of personal growth and purpose

Grandmaster Miller's message is clear: **leadership is a daily discipline. Excellence is a decision. Legacy is intentional**.

I have had the opportunity to work with leaders across industries, from university programs to corporate environments, and I can confidently say that the principles outlined in this book are universal. They are timeless. And when applied, they produce results.

This book will challenge you to think differently. It will challenge you to act with greater intention. And most importantly, it will challenge you to become the standard—not just follow one.

Grandmaster Stephen Miller has not only written a book—he has delivered a call to action. As you turn these pages, I encourage you to read with an open mind, reflect with honesty, and most importantly—apply what you learn. Because knowledge without action is wasted potential, and leadership without execution is merely conversation.

On behalf of the martial arts community, the leadership community, and those committed to excellence, I commend Grandmaster Miller for this outstanding contribution. Your journey to higher levels of leadership, influence, and impact *begins now.*

Yours in the Martial Arts,
Dr. Jessie Bowen
10th Degree Black Belt
Elite Publications, Founder
Author, Speaker & Leadership Strategist
"Everyone has a story—you just have to get it out."

ACKNOWLEDGEMENTS

No journey of leadership is walked alone. This book reflects my experiences and the countless individuals who have shaped, challenged, and strengthened me. I am deeply grateful to all who have contributed to my growth as a martial artist, business leader, and man of purpose.

First and foremost, I give thanks to God for the strength, wisdom, and guidance that have carried me through every season of life. In moments of uncertainty, it has been my faith that has grounded me, and in moments of success, it has reminded me to remain humble and grateful.

To my instructors and martial arts mentors, thank you for teaching discipline, respect, and perseverance. The lessons learned on the training floor shaped my character and my leadership. Your standards pushed me to improve as both a martial artist and a leader.

To my students, you have often been my greatest teachers. Your growth and commitment remind me of the responsibilities of leadership. Seeing your development has been a rewarding part of my journey.

To my colleagues and team members, thank you for your trust and collaboration. Leadership in business requires vision and unity. Together, we have faced challenges and celebrated victories. Your dedication inspires me.

To my wife Robin, your unwavering support has been my foundation. Leadership often demands sacrifice, and your encouragement has allowed me to pursue my calling with determination. I am deeply grateful for your love and belief in me.

I also acknowledge those who may not realize their impact—the individuals who led by example and demonstrated integrity and resilience. Leadership is often taught in quiet moments, and I carry those lessons forward.

Finally, to you, the reader, thank you for taking this journey. Your commitment to growth and to becoming a better version of yourself gives this work its true purpose. Leadership is not about standing above others; it is about lifting others up. If this book helps you do that, then its mission has been fulfilled.

THE INFLUENCE OF CONFIDENCE, DISCIPLINE & RESPECT IN LEADERSHIP

INTRODUCTION

My journey began not with mastery, but with a decision — to step onto the mat and commit to a path that would challenge me physically, mentally, and spiritually. Over the years, that path evolved more than training. It became a system of thinking, a standard of living, and a framework for leadership.

Through decades of martial arts practice, instruction, and mentorship, I have trained students from all walks of life, young beginners seeking confidence, competitors striving for excellence, and leaders looking to sharpen their edge. In every environment, one truth has remained constant:

The principles that build a great martial artist are the same principles that build a great leader.

My experience extends beyond the dojang into the world of business, where I have worked with executives, entrepreneurs, and organizations seeking structure, clarity, and sustainable growth. I have seen firsthand how discipline translates into execution, how confidence drives decision-making, and how respect builds powerful teams.

Where many separate martial arts and business, I have spent my life integrating them.

Because at their core, both require:

- Strategic thinking under pressure
- Consistent execution over time
- Emotional control in high-stakes environments
- The ability to lead others toward a shared vision

As a martial arts instructor, I teach individuals how to master themselves. As a business expert, I teach leaders how to build systems that scale beyond themselves.

But at the highest level, my mission is clear: to develop warrior-leaders who lead with confidence, act with discipline, and influence with respect.

This book is not theory. It is the result of lived experience, tested principles, and decades of application in both martial arts and business environments...

Respectfully,

Grandmaster Stephen Miller
7th Degree Black Belt
Instructor, Author & Business Strategist

CHAPTER 1
The Warrior-Leader Paradigm

Leadership, on the training floor or in the boardroom, is not a title but a responsibility forged by character, tested by adversity, and proven by consistent action. Through my journey as a martial artist and business manager, I've found three principles that define lasting leadership: **confidence, discipline, and respect**.

These are not abstract ideas; they are living principles—practiced daily, refined by failure, and strengthened by experience. A black belt is not earned overnight. It takes years of repetition, sacrifice, humility, and growth. Leadership follows the same path.

A leader without confidence *hesitates*.
A leader without discipline *falters*.
A leader without respect *fails*.

To summarize, confidence, discipline, and respect enable a leader to guide others with positive influence. Remember: true impact begins with these pillars.

1st Pillar: Confidence–The Foundation of Conviction

Confidence is the cornerstone of leadership, enabling decisive action, clear communication, and trust, even in the face of uncertainty.

As stated in my foundational framework on leadership development, confidence is not the absence of doubt but the disciplined ability to act in spite of it.

Understanding True Confidence

Confidence is built, not given. It comes from preparation, is sharpened by adversity, and is proved by action. In martial arts, repetition develops confidence—a technique practiced often becomes instinct. The same applies in business, where repeated challenges build a leader's clarity and composure.

True confidence is rooted in:
- **Competence**–mastery of skills and knowledge
- **Preparation**–readiness for expected and unexpected challenges
- **Self-trust**–belief in one's ability to adapt and respond

A confident leader does not claim perfection. Instead, they trust their ability to navigate imperfection.

Confidence vs. Arrogance

One of the most critical distinctions a leader must understand is the difference between confidence and arrogance. Confidence is grounded in purpose. Arrogance is rooted in insecurity. A confident leader listens, adapts, and collaborates. An arrogant leader dismisses, controls, and isolates.

In both martial arts and business:
- Confidence builds teams
- Arrogance breaks them

The leader who commands respect is not the loudest voice in the room, but the most consistent presence.

The Components of Confidence

Confidence is not a single trait—it is a composite of several key elements:

1. **Self-Awareness:** A leader must understand their strengths, weaknesses, values, and motivations. Without self-awareness, confidence becomes unstable.
2. **Preparation:** Preparation reduces uncertainty. A prepared leader does not fear challenges—they anticipate them.

3. **Resilience:** Confidence is tested in adversity. The ability to recover, adapt, and continue forward defines true strength.
4. **Integrity:** Confidence without integrity is fragile. When actions align with values, trust is established.
5. **Presence:** Confidence is shown nonverbally—through posture, tone, and composure. A calm leader brings stability.

The Leadership Advantage of Confidence

Confidence enables leaders to:
- Make decisive choices under pressure.
- Inspire trust and credibility.
- Empower teams to act independently.
- Maintain stability during a crisis.
- Encourage innovation and calculated risk.

Teams follow conviction, not titles. Confidence sets the tone for performance.

2nd Pillar: Discipline–The Structure of Excellence

If confidence is the foundation, discipline is the structure that sustains leadership.

Discipline bridges intention and execution. It means committing to standards daily, even when motivation fades.

In martial arts, discipline is evident in every bow, every stance, every repetition. In business, it is reflected in consistency, accountability, and execution.

The Nature of Discipline

Discipline is not punishment, it is alignment. It aligns:
- Actions with goals
- Behavior with values
- Effort with outcomes

A disciplined leader does what is needed, regardless of mood, convenience, or circumstance.

The Role of Discipline in Leadership

Leadership without discipline is unpredictable. Teams require stability, and discipline provides it. A disciplined leader:
- Sets clear expectations
- Follows through on commitments
- Maintains standards under pressure
- Models consistency

In martial arts or business, inconsistency breeds doubt. Discipline removes it.

Daily Discipline: The Leader's Routine

Effective leaders build discipline through habits and structured routines that fuel productivity and clarity. These include:

- Morning preparation–setting intentions and priorities
- Focused execution–eliminating distractions
- Continuous learning–refining skills daily
- Reflection–evaluating outcomes and adjusting strategies

Success comes from consistent discipline, not occasional effort.

Discipline Under Pressure

True discipline is revealed when circumstances become difficult.

When *fatigue* sets in…
When *obstacles* arise…
When *results* are delayed…
The disciplined leader continues.

Martial artists don't skip training because it is hard. Difficulty is the training. Leadership is the same.

The Consequences of Undisciplined Leadership

Without discipline:

- Goals become unclear
- Teams lose direction
- Performance declines
- Trust erodes

In conclusion, discipline is essential for achieving clear goals, maintaining direction, and establishing rapport. Without it, trust and performance dissolve.

3rd Pillar: Respect–The Currency of Leadership

Respect is the most powerful and often most misunderstood principle in leadership. It cannot be demanded. It must be earned.

In martial arts, respect is foundational. It is demonstrated before and after every interaction. It is not a sign of weakness—it is a sign of strength.

Understanding Respect in Leadership

Respect starts with self-respect. Leaders who don't value their standards can't expect others to follow them. From there, respect extends outward:

- Respect for individuals
- Respect for roles
- Respect for the mission

Respect creates connection; without it, leadership is transactional.

Respect vs. Authority

A leader may have authority, but without respect, influence is limited. Respect is built through:

- Consistency
- Fairness
- Listening
- Accountability

The leader who respects their team earns loyalty. The leader who demands obedience without respect earns resistance.

Creating a Culture of Respect

Leadership is not just about individual behavior. It is about creating an environment. A culture of respect:

- Encourages open communication
- Values diverse perspectives
- Promotes psychological safety
- Strengthens collaboration

In these environments, people perform their best—not out of fear, but commitment.

Respect in Conflict

Conflict is inevitable in leadership. Respect determines how it is managed. A respectful leader:

- Addresses issues directly
- Listens before responding
- Focuses on solutions rather than blame

In martial arts, control means precision, not domination. Leadership follows this principle.

*KEY TAKEAWAY: Authority can be given, but respect must be earned. Sustainable influence is built by consistent, respectful actions.

The Integration of Confidence, Discipline, and Respect

Individually, each principle is powerful. Together, they are transformative:

- Confidence provides direction
- Discipline ensures execution
- Respect sustains relationships

A leader who embodies all three creates an environment where:

- Teams trust leadership
- Goals are consistently achieved.
- Growth becomes inevitable

The Leadership Triangle

These principles form a balanced structure:

- **Confidence without discipline** leads to inconsistency.
- **Discipline without respect** leads to rigidity.
- **Respect without confidence** leads to indecision.

To lead effectively, integrate all three principles—confidence, discipline, and respect. This holistic approach forms the core leadership takeaway.

Practical Application in Martial Arts and Business

Scenario 1: The Martial Arts Instructor

An instructor leading a class must:

- Demonstrate confidence in teaching techniques.
- Maintain discipline in structure and expectations.
- Show respect to every student, regardless of level.

The result: a class that is focused, motivated, and engaged.

Scenario 2: The Business Executive

An executive managing a team must:

- Make confident decisions under uncertainty.
- Enforce disciplined processes.
- Foster a culture of respect.

***KEY TAKEAWAY**: leadership grounded in confidence, discipline, and respect produces teams built on trust, accountability, and high performance.

Developing the Leader Within

Leadership is not static—it is a continuous process of growth. To develop these principles:

1. **Commit to Growth:** Step outside comfort zones. Growth requires challenge.
2. **Seek Mentorship:** Learn from those who have walked the path.
3. **Practice Reflection:** Evaluate actions, decisions, and outcomes.
4. **Build Habits:** Consistency creates discipline. Discipline builds confidence.
5. **Lead by Example:** In practice, demonstrate leadership through consistent action. The core lesson: lead by example for lasting impact.

The Legacy of Leadership

In martial arts, we often speak of legacy—not in terms of titles or accolades, but in terms of impact. The same is true in leadership. Your legacy isn't what you achieve, but what you inspire in others.

Confidence will determine how you *lead*.
Discipline will determine how you *sustain*.
Respect will determine how you are *remembered*.

Leadership is not about control, but influence. It guides others toward a vision, helps them face challenges, and empowers growth.

As I have learned throughout my journey, leadership is not a destination. It is a path—a disciplined, intentional, and purposeful path.

And like the martial artist who steps onto the mat each day, the leader must commit to the process.

Train your mind.
Strengthen your discipline.
Honor others with respect.

In doing so, you will not only lead—*you will inspire.*

CHAPTER 2
The Warrior-Leader Standard

Leadership is not accidental. It is not a title or position. Leadership is earned by consistency, tested by adversity, and proven by action.

Too often, leadership is misunderstood as something granted—something that comes with promotion, recognition, or authority. Yet, in both the dojang and the boardroom, I have observed a different reality. Titles may designate responsibility, but they do not guarantee effectiveness. Authority may establish a position, but it does not ensure influence.

In over four decades of training martial artists, coaching executives, and working at the highest levels of business and organizational development, I have come to understand a universal truth: **Leadership is not built on authority is built on alignment of character.**

This alignment isn't accidental. It's developed, refined, and tested through experiences challenging both competence and conviction.

A leader's character shows not during comfort, but in uncertainty—when decisions are unclear, outcomes unknown, and pressure high. The leader relies on who they are, not their role.

That identity—strong, grounded, and effective—is built upon three foundational pillars:

- Confidence–the ability to act with clarity and conviction
- Discipline–the ability to execute consistently regardless of circumstance
- Respect–the ability to connect, influence, and elevate others

***KEY TAKEAWAY**: Confidence, discipline, and respect are essential to stable and effective leadership. Without them, leadership loses its foundation, focus, and impact.

The Foundation of the Warrior-Leader

In martial arts, we train bodies to act under pressure. Techniques are drilled until instinctive. Movements are refined until they're automatic. In confrontation, there's no time to think—only to act. The same principle applies to leadership.

In business, we train minds for uncertainty. Markets shift. Conditions change. Variables multiply. Leaders must assess, decide, and act—often without full information.

Yet beyond both physical training and intellectual preparation lies something deeper: **Character**.

Character is what allows a leader to remain steady when everything else is not.

It prevents *panic under pressure.*
It sustains *focus amid distractions.*
It guides *decisions when outcomes are unclear.*

A leader may possess knowledge, but without character, that knowledge becomes ineffective. A leader may possess authority, but without character, that authority becomes fragile.

The warrior-leader understands that leadership is not about reacting to circumstances, it is about mastering oneself within those circumstances.

Confidence: The Inner Authority

Confidence is leadership's first pillar; it underpins all action. Without confidence, decisions stall. Opportunities are lost. Teams drift.

However, confidence must be understood correctly. It is not arrogance, dominance, or the loudest voice. True confidence is quiet. It is steady. It is grounded in preparation and experience.

In martial arts, confidence is not given—it is earned. A student gains confidence not through encouragement alone, but through repetition, correction, and persistence. They fall. They adjust. They improve. Over time, their belief in themselves becomes rooted in experience. Leadership takes the same path.

Confidence is cultivated through:
- Preparation
- Action
- Reflection
- Resilience

A confident leader does not require certainty to act. They require clarity of purpose.

They understand that:
- Not every decision will be perfect
- Not every outcome will be favorable
- Not every situation will be predictable

Yet they act anyway.

*KEY TAKEAWAY: True confidence means moving forward despite doubt, trusting one's preparation, and maintaining clarity in purpose.

Discipline: The Standard of Execution

If confidence is the foundation, discipline sustains it. Discipline is commitment to consistency—the ability to perform in any situation.

In martial arts, discipline turns practice into mastery. A technique repeated once is understood. Repeated thousands of times, it becomes instinct.

In leadership, discipline transforms vision into results. Many leaders have ideas. Fewer have execution. Discipline separates the two.

A disciplined leader:
- Shows up prepared
- Follows through on commitments
- Maintains standards under pressure
- Executes consistently over time

They do not depend on motivation. They rely on structure. Motivation fluctuates. Discipline endures.

In both martial arts and business, there is a principle that cannot be ignored: **You do not rise to your expectations. You fall to your level of discipline**.

This means that during pressure, uncertainty, or challenge, a leader will not perform based on intention. They will perform based on habit. Discipline creates those habits.

It ensures that:
- Standards are maintained
- Systems are followed
- Results are achieved

***KEY TAKEAWAY**: Discipline ensures confidence is reliable. With commitment, habits, and standards, leaders deliver results even under pressure.

Respect: The Power of Connection

The third pillar—respect—is what transforms leadership from control to influence. Respect is often mistaken for politeness or courtesy. In reality, it is much more.

Respect is:
- Recognition of value
- Acknowledgment of contribution
- Commitment to fairness

It is the foundation of trust.

Without respect, leadership is only transactional. People comply because they must—not because they believe.

With respect, leadership is transformational. People engage, contribute, and grow.

In martial arts, respect is foundational:
- Respect for the instructor
- Respect for training partners
- Respect for the art itself

This respect-driven culture fosters growth. In leadership, the same principle applies.

A respected leader:
- Listens actively
- Communicates clearly
- Acts with integrity
- Treats others with dignity

They understand that leadership is not about elevating oneself—it is about elevating others.

Respect builds:
- Trust
- Loyalty
- Collaboration

Without respect, even skilled leaders lose influence. Respect builds trust and team contribution, making growth and transformation possible.

The Integration of the Three Pillars

Confidence, discipline, and respect do not work alone. They form an integrated system.

- *Confidence* provides direction
- *Discipline* provides execution
- *Respect* provides connection

Remove one, and the system weakens:
Confidence without discipline leads to inconsistency.
Discipline without respect leads to rigidity.
Respect without confidence leads to passivity.

***KEY TAKEAWAY**: The warrior-leader builds confidence, discipline, and respect together to drive lasting, effective leadership.

Leadership Under Pressure

Pressure is the proving ground of leadership.

It is easy to lead when conditions are favorable. It is easy to communicate when outcomes are predictable. It is easy to remain composed when there is no resistance. But leadership is not measured in ease. It is measured in challenge.

In martial arts, pressure reveals preparation. When a student faces resistance, their training is exposed. If their foundation is weak, it becomes evident. If their preparation is strong, it becomes undeniable. The same is true in leadership.

Under pressure:
- Confidence is tested
- Discipline is revealed
- Respect is demonstrated

A leader who lacks confidence *hesitates*.
A leader who lacks discipline *falters*.
A leader who lacks respect *loses trust*.

***KEY TAKEAWAY**: A leader grounded in confidence, discipline, and respect remains steady during challenges and inspires others.

The Warrior-Leader Mindset

The warrior-leader does not wait for the right conditions.
They do not wait for certainty.
They do not wait for approval.
They do not wait for perfect timing.
They act.

This does not mean reckless action. It means prepared action. It means intentional movement forward—even when conditions are imperfect.

The warrior-leader understands that:
- Conditions will never be perfect
- Challenges will always exist
- Uncertainty is constant

Therefore, they do not depend on external stability. They develop internal stability.

***KEY TAKEAWAY**: By developing internal stability, leaders set the standard others aspire to follow, guiding teams through uncertain times.

Becoming the Standard

To become the standard means:
- Maintaining composure when others react
- Acting decisively when others hesitate
- Upholding integrity when others compromise

***KEY TAKEAWAY**: True leadership is shown through example. Actions, not words, shape teams and values in any organization.

In martial arts, the instructor demonstrates before the student performs. In leadership, the same principle applies.

Your actions:
- Set the tone
- Define expectations
- Shape culture

People do not follow what *you say*.
They follow what *you do*.

The Responsibility of Leadership

Leadership is not a privilege—it is a responsibility. Every decision:

- Impacts others
- Influences outcomes
- Shapes direction

A leader must be intentional. They must understand that their behavior:

- Sets standards
- Creates culture
- Builds or breaks trust

***KEY TAKEAWAY**: The decisions you make and the standards you uphold build trust, shape outcomes, and define your leadership legacy.

The Path Forward

The journey of leadership is continuous. There is no final destination—only continual refinement.

Each day presents an opportunity to:

- Strengthen confidence
- Reinforce discipline
- Demonstrate respect

Each challenge presents an opportunity to grow.

***KEY TAKEAWAY**: Leadership is ongoing. Each decision offers a chance to grow and further develop your leadership identity.

Leadership is not about position—it is about presence.
It is not about *control*—it is about *influence*.
It is not about *authority*—it is about *alignment of character*.

Confidence gives you the courage to act.
Discipline gives you the ability to execute.
Respect gives you the power to lead others.

Together, they form the foundation of the warrior-leader.
And the warrior-leader does not wait for the right conditions.

The warrior-leader becomes the standard—regardless of conditions.

CHAPTER 3

Projecting Confidence Without Dominance

Confidence is the foundation of conviction. Confidence is a defining trait of leadership, yet it must be expressed with precision, discipline, and awareness.

Over the course of my journey—as both a martial artist and a business consultant—I have observed a critical distinction that separates effective leaders from ineffective ones: **Confidence, when unrefined, can easily be mistaken for dominance**.

This misunderstanding has cost many leaders their influence, teams, and legacy. True leadership elevates others, not overpowers. It establishes trust, not just control.

As stated earlier: confidence without discipline and respect is often seen as dominance. True leadership requires presence, not force.

This chapter expands upon that principle and provides a deeper exploration into how leaders can project confidence in a way that inspires, stabilizes, and empowers—without ever diminishing those around them.

***KEY TAKEAWAY**: Project confidence through presence, not control, to foster trust and growth.

The Misinterpretation of Confidence

In both the dojang and the boardroom, I have seen individuals attempt to "look confident" by increasing their volume, asserting authority prematurely, or dominating conversations. These behaviors may generate temporary compliance—but they rarely produce long-term respect.

Dominance is often rooted in insecurity. When leaders feel uncertain internally, they compensate externally. They attempt to control the environment rather than master themselves. This creates tension, resistance, and, eventually, disengagement among those they lead.

Confidence, by contrast, is internal alignment. It is not about being seen—it is about being steady.

A confident leader:
- Does not need to prove their capability
- Does not rely on intimidation to gain compliance
- Does not fear opposing viewpoints

Instead, they remain centered. Their strength is evident, not announced.

In martial arts, a true black belt does not walk into a room seeking validation. Their presence alone communicates discipline, training, and control. The same principle applies to leadership.

The Power of Presence

Presence is one of the most overlooked yet powerful tools in leadership. Before you speak, before you act, before you give direction—your presence has already communicated something to those around you. Posture, composure, and awareness all shape perception.

As emphasized: a leader who carries themselves with composure, clarity, and intention communicates confidence without ever raising their voice.

Presence is not *accidental*—it is *trained*.

The Three Elements of Leadership Presence

Element 1: Physical Alignment:
Your body reflects your mindset: slouched posture signals uncertainty, rigid posture tension, balanced posture control. A leader should stand:
- Upright, but relaxed
- Grounded, yet fluid
- Still, but ready

This mirrors martial arts stance—stable, but adaptable.

Element 2: Mental Clarity:
A distracted leader cannot project confidence. When your thoughts are scattered, your communication becomes inconsistent. Clarity arises from preparation, discipline, and focus. Before entering any leadership situation, ask:

* What is the objective?
* What outcome am I guiding toward?
* What energy must I bring?

Element 3: Emotional Control:

Your emotional state becomes the emotional environment of your team. If you are reactive, your team becomes anxious. If you are composed, your team becomes stable. *Calmness is not passive, it is powerful.*

Communication: The Reflection of Inner Discipline

Leadership communication extends far beyond words. In fact, as highlighted: leadership communication goes far beyond words—the method of communication frequently outweighs the message itself. This principle is critical.

***KEY TAKEAWAY**: How you communicate is often more influential than what you say.

Non-Verbal Communication: The Silent Authority

Your non-verbal communication is your first language. Before you speak, people observe:

- How you carry yourself
- How you look at others
- How you respond to pressure

These signals determine whether people trust you.

Key Non-Verbal Elements:
- **Eye Contact**: Confidence is expressed through steady, respectful eye contact—not avoidance, not intimidation.
- **Facial Expression**: A composed expression shows emotional control. Overreaction signals instability.
- **Movement**: Controlled movement reflects controlled thinking. Erratic gestures suggest uncertainty.
- **Stillness**: Stillness, is strength. In martial arts, unnecessary movement wastes energy. In leadership, unnecessary motion weakens authority.

Verbal Communication: Authority with Precision

A disciplined leader speaks with intention. Leaders are not judged by how much they say, but by how well they are understood. This is a principle I emphasize in executive coaching.

Effective Verbal Leadership Includes:
- Clarity over complexity
- Direction without aggression
- Confidence without arrogance

Instead of saying: *"This is what we're doing. No discussion."*
Say: *"Here is the direction I recommend, and here's why."* This invites alignment rather than resistance.

Ownership Language is essential:
- "I believe…"
- "I recommend…"
- "Let's move forward with…"

This communicates leadership without force.

The Balance Between Confidence and Humility

One of the greatest leadership paradoxes is this: confidence and humility must coexist. Confidence without humility creates distance. Humility without confidence creates doubt. Together, they create trust. This balance defines mature leadership.

***KEY TAKEAWAY**: Effective leaders blend confidence with humility to build trust.

Confidence Without Humility

Leaders who lack humility:
- Dismiss input
- Resist correction
- Seek validation of the results.

This creates *disconnection*.

Humility Without Confidence

Leaders who lack confidence:
- Hesitate in decision-making
- Avoid responsibility
- Fail to inspire direction.

This creates *uncertainty*.

The Integrated Leader

The strongest leaders:
- Listen without losing authority
- Lead without losing perspective
- Decide without ego

Humility is not weakness—it is awareness. In martial arts, even a master continues to learn. The moment learning stops, growth ends.

Calm Strength: The Leadership Advantage

In a world that often equates leadership with loudness, calm strength stands apart. As emphasized: calm strength is one of the most powerful forms of leadership.

Calm strength is the ability to:
- Remain composed under pressure
- Think clearly in chaos
- Act decisively without emotional reaction

Why Calm Strength Works

People do not follow panic. They follow stability. During adversity, your team is not just listening to your words—they are watching your reactions.

If you remain calm:
- You create confidence
- You reduce fear
- You maintain direction

In martial arts, panic leads to mistakes. Calmness leads to precision. The same applies in leadership.

Confidence That Empowers Others

Leadership is not about control—it is about development. Your role is not to create followers—it is to develop leaders. This is a fundamental shift in perspective.

***KEY TAKEAWAY**: Empower others to lead, not just follow.

Dominant Leadership vs Empowered Leadership

Dominant Leadership:
- Controls decisions
- Limits input
- Creates dependency

Empowered Leadership:
- Encourages contribution
- Builds confidence in others
- Develops future leaders

When confidence is expressed through dominance:
- Creativity declines
- Communication weakens
- Trust erodes

When confidence is expressed through respect:
- Innovation increases
- Engagement improves
- Performance strengthens

Practical Leadership Behaviors

Effective leadership is not theoretical—it is demonstrated through behavior. As observed: the most effective leaders consistently demonstrate disciplined, respectful actions.

Core Behaviors of Confident Leaders
1. **Listening Before Responding:** Listening demonstrates control. Interrupting demonstrates insecurity.

2. **Acknowledging Contributions:** Recognition builds morale. Ignoring input weakens trust.
3. **Correcting with Dignity:** Correction should develop—not diminish.
4. **Taking Responsibility:** Leaders own failures and distribute success.
5. **Maintaining Consistency:** Inconsistency creates confusion. Consistency builds credibility.

***KEY TAKEAWAY**: Consistent actions establish your reliability as a leader.

Self-Awareness: The Discipline Behind Confidence

Confidence without self-awareness becomes arrogance. Self-awareness requires reflection. You must constantly evaluate your intentions and impact as a leader.

Reflective Questions for Leaders
- *Am I leading to serve others or to elevate myself?*
- *Am I listening to understand or to respond?*
- *Am I building trust or demanding compliance?*

These questions are not optional—they are essential. Growth begins with awareness.

***KEY TAKEAWAY**: Self-awareness lays the groundwork for effective, humble leadership.

Case Study: The Executive vs The Instructor

Allow me to illustrate this principle through experience.

Scenario 1: The Executive Leader

An executive enters a meeting with authority, speaks over others, dismisses feedback, and enforces decisions without discussion.

Result:
- Immediate compliance
- Long-term disengagement
- Reduced innovation

Scenario 2: The Martial Arts Instructor

An instructor enters calmly, observes the room, listens, provides direction with clarity, and encourages participation.

Result:
- Immediate respect
- Long-term commitment
- Continuous improvement

The difference is not *knowledge*—it is *delivery*.

***KEY TAKEAWAY**: Leadership impact depends on how you engage, not just what you know.

The Leadership Standard

Projecting confidence without dominance requires:
- Discipline
- Awareness
- Intentional communication
- Respect for others

It is not easy—but it is necessary. The most respected leaders are remembered not for how loud they were, but for how they made others feel. This is the ultimate measure of leadership.

*KEY TAKEAWAY: Great leaders are defined by their positive impact on others.

Final Reflection

Confidence, when guided by discipline and respect, becomes a force that transforms organizations, teams, and individuals. It:
- Builds trust
- Strengthens culture
- Creates lasting impact

Leadership is not about standing above others. It is about standing strong—so others can rise. Because in the end, the true measure of leadership is not how many follow you…

It is how many grow because of you.

CHAPTER 4

Discipline as a Leadership Habit: The Engine of Consistency Part I

Discipline is a defining—yet misunderstood—quality of leadership. Through decades of training martial artists, developing leaders, and consulting in business, I learned one truth: **Discipline does not start success—it sustains it.**

Vision will inspire. Confidence will initiate. But discipline moves a leader forward when inspiration fades and confidence wavers.

Many aspire to lead. Few are willing to discipline themselves to lead consistently.

Leadership is not proven in moments of excitement. It is proven in moments of resistance. It's easy to perform when conditions are ideal, motivation is high, recognition is present, and results are immediate. True leadership is revealed when these conditions are absent.

Can you remain steady when progress is slow?
Can you remain focused when distractions are constant?

Can you remain committed when results are uncertain?

This is the domain of discipline. And here, leadership is forged.

Understanding Discipline: The Alignment of Action and Purpose

Discipline is often seen as restrictive. Many view it as rigid or confining. In reality, it is not. Discipline means alignment.

It is the alignment of:
- Actions with values
- Decisions with purpose
- Behavior with standards

A disciplined leader is not impulsive. They act with intention. They understand the difference between:
- Urgency and importance
- Emotion and logic
- Ego and mission

This awareness separates *reactive* from *intentional* leadership.

In martial arts, we train not just for physical mastery, but for control—control of movement, control of timing, and ultimately, control of self. Leadership requires the same self-control.

The greatest opponent a leader will ever face is not external—it is internal. Undisciplined thinking leads to inconsistent action. Inconsistent action leads to unreliable results. Unreliable results erode trust. And without trust, leadership cannot exist.

Discipline as a Daily Practice, Not an Occasional Effort

One of the greatest misconceptions about discipline is this: It is something you "turn on" when needed. It is not. Discipline is a habit, not an act. It is built daily, through small decisions that often go unnoticed:

- Choosing preparation over procrastination
- Choosing structure over chaos
- Choosing consistency over convenience

In martial arts training, we do not practice techniques only when we feel motivated. We train regardless of how we feel. Why? Because we understand that consistency builds mastery. The same principle applies in leadership.

A leader who waits for motivation is inconsistent. A leader who operates with discipline will always be dependable.

Dependability builds *trust*.
Trust builds *influence*.
Influence builds *leadership*.

The Paradox of Discipline: Structure Creates Freedom

There is a paradox that many fail to understand: **Discipline creates freedom.**

Without discipline:
- Time is wasted
- Energy is scattered
- Focus is lost

With discipline:
- Time is structured
- Energy is directed
- Focus is intentional

In business, I have seen leaders overwhelmed not because they lacked ability, but because they lacked structure.

They *reacted* instead of *planning*.
They *responded* instead of *leading*.
They *managed chaos* instead of *creating clarity*.

Discipline removes chaos. It allows leaders to:
- Focus on what truly matters.
- Eliminate unnecessary distractions
- Build systems that support long-term success.

Freedom is not found in doing whatever you want. Freedom is found in having the discipline to do what matters most.

The Four Pillars of Disciplined Leadership

Through years of experience, I have identified four foundational traits. These traits define disciplined leadership. They are not theoretical. They are practical, observable, and essential.

Pillar 1: Consistency of Character

Leadership begins with identity. Who you are determines how you lead. A disciplined leader maintains consistency regardless of the environment. They do not adjust their values based on audience or circumstance.

They are the same:
- In private and in public
- In success and in failure
- In pressure and in peace

This consistency creates *predictability*.
And predictability builds *trust*.

When people know what to expect from you, they begin to rely on your leadership. They align with your standards. They follow your example.

In martial arts, your stance must remain stable regardless of your opponent's movement. In leadership, your character must remain stable regardless of external conditions.

Pillar 2: Relentless Follow-Through

Words may inspire, but actions establish credibility. A disciplined leader does what they say. They:
- Honor commitments
- Meet deadlines
- Complete what they begin.

This is not about *perfection*, but *reliability*.

In business, I have seen organizations fail, not because of poor ideas. They fail because of poor execution. Ideas without discipline remain unrealized. Execution requires follow-through.

When a leader consistently follows through:
- Teams become accountable

- Standards become clear
- Performance improves

A leader who does not follow through teaches their team that commitments are optional. A disciplined leader teaches that commitments are non-negotiable.

Pillar 3: Focus on What Matters Most

In today's world, distraction is constant. Opportunities, demands, and responsibilities compete for attention. They do so at every level. Without discipline, leaders become reactive. They chase urgency, not impact. A disciplined leader protects their focus. They:
- Prioritize high-impact activities
- Delegate effectively
- Say no when necessary.
- Align actions with long-term objectives.

Focus is never accidental; it's intentional.

In martial arts, a single moment of distraction can determine the outcome of a match. In leadership, a lack of focus can determine an organization's outcome. Where attention goes, results follow.

Pillar 4: Resilience Through Adversity

Discipline is most visible when circumstances are most difficult. Anyone can lead when conditions are favorable. But leadership is revealed in adversity.

A disciplined leader:
- Controls emotions under pressure

- Adapts without compromising values
- Continues forward despite obstacles

In martial arts, resilience comes from repeated challenge. We do not avoid difficulty—we train through it. Leadership requires the same mindset. Adversity doesn't interrupt leadership. It is a test of it.

Structure, Routines, and Standards: The Framework of Discipline

Leadership without structure leads to inconsistency. Discipline requires systems. A strong leader builds three essential frameworks:

1. **Structure**:
Structure provides clarity. It defines:
   - Roles
   - Responsibilities
   - Processes

Without structure, confusion grows. With structure, efficiency improves.

2. **Routines**:
Routines create rhythm. They establish:
   - Daily habits
   - Weekly priorities
   - Consistent actions

Routines reduce decision fatigue and increase productivity. They let leaders work with clarity, not chaos.

3. **Standards**:
Standards define excellence. They communicate:

❖ What is acceptable
❖ What is expected
❖ What is required

A disciplined leader does not lower standards to accommodate inconsistency. They raise performance to meet standards.

Disciplined Decision-Making: Leadership Under Pressure

Decision-making is one of the greatest tests of leadership. Under pressure, undisciplined leaders *react*. Disciplined leaders *respond*.

They approach decisions with:
- Patience
- Clarity
- Strategic thinking

They assess immediate and long-term impacts. They understand that leadership decisions must align with principles—not emotions.

In martial arts, reacting too quickly often leads to mistakes. The disciplined practitioner observes, analyzes, and responds with precision. Leadership requires the same control.

Execution: Where Discipline Becomes Reality

Vision without execution is an illusion. Discipline is what transforms ideas into results.

A disciplined leader:
- Breaks goals into actionable steps

- Tracks progress consistently
- Adjusts without losing direction
- Holds themselves and others accountable

Execution is about consistency, not intensity. Small, disciplined actions repeated over time produce extraordinary results.

In both martial arts and business, success is not determined by how you start. It is determined by how you sustain.

The Cultural Impact of Discipline

Discipline is not limited to the individual leader. It shapes organizational culture.

A disciplined leader creates:
- A culture of accountability
- A culture of consistency
- A culture of excellence

People do not follow words—they follow examples. When leaders embody discipline:
- Teams adopt discipline
- Standards rise
- Performance improves

Culture results from behavior, not intention. It is created by behavior.

The Legacy of Discipline

Discipline's greatest impact is often unseen. It does not seek recognition. It does not demand attention.

Yet it produces:

- Trust through consistency
- Respect through integrity
- Results through persistence

A disciplined leader does more than achieve goals.
They build systems that *endure*.
They create standards that *outlive them*.
They influence others to rise to a *higher level*.

This is the true measure of leadership.

Final Reflection: Discipline as Identity

Discipline is not applied. It is something you become. When discipline becomes a habit:

- Leadership becomes consistent
- Performance becomes reliable
- Influence becomes lasting

In martial arts, we say: *"You do not rise to the level of your expectations—you fall to the level of your training."* In leadership, the same principle applies. You do not rise to the level of your ambition. You fall to the level of your discipline. And that is why discipline is not optional.

It is essential.

Closing Statement

Discipline bridges the gap between intention and achievement.

It is the quiet force behind *every effective leader.*
It is the structure behind *every successful organization.*
It is the habit that transforms *potential into performance.*

And for those who choose to embody it—it becomes the foundation of lasting leadership.

CHAPTER 5

Self-Discipline and Personal Accountability: The Engine of Consistency Part II

Leadership starts with the discipline you require of yourself and how you lead by example.

During my journey in martial arts and business, I have learned that the most effective leaders are not those who simply instruct, but those who embody. Your actions, habits, and standards become the blueprint others follow. Whether you realize it or not, every decision you make is being observed, interpreted, and often replicated.

Leadership is not only about what you say—it is about what you consistently do.

The Responsibility to Model Behavior

One of the greatest responsibilities of leadership is setting the standard through personal example. You cannot expect discipline from your team if you do not demonstrate it yourself. You cannot require accountability if you are unwilling to hold yourself accountable.

Leadership is not enforced through authority—it is established through consistency.

A disciplined leader:
- Shows up prepared and on time
- Honors commitments regardless of convenience
- Maintains calmness under pressure
- Demonstrates humility in both success and failure

These behaviors are not just symbolic; they are foundational. They show your team what is acceptable and expected.

When leaders fail to exhibit these standards, confusion and mistrust result. But when leaders lead by example, alignment occurs naturally.

Self-Discipline in Daily Practice

Self-discipline is not built in a single moment of strength—it is developed through daily habits. It is revealed in how you manage your time, regulate your emotions, and prioritize long-term success over short-term comfort.

Time Management: Leading with Purpose

Time is one of the most valuable resources a leader possesses. Disciplined leaders do not allow their time to be controlled by pressure or distraction. They operate with intention. They:
- Determine clear priorities
- Structure their day around high-impact activities.
- Protect their time from unnecessary interruptions.
- Delegate effectively to preserve focus on leadership responsibilities.

Effective time management creates organizational rhythm, reduces chaos, and improves productivity. Time discipline is not about doing more—it is about doing what matters most.

Self-Regulation: Mastering Emotional Control

Leadership will test your emotional discipline. In pressure, conflict, and uncertainty, your response defines your leadership.

Disciplined leaders:
- Pause before reacting
- Maintain a steady tone and presence.
- Respond with clarity rather than emotion.
- Create space for careful decision-making.

Emotional control is not suppression—it is mastery. A composed leader inspires confidence; impulsive reactions cause instability. Your emotional discipline sets the emotional standard for your organization.

Delayed Gratification: The Long-Term Mindset

In leadership, the greatest rewards are rarely immediate. Self-discipline requires the ability to delay gratification—to choose long-term impact instead of short-term comfort. This means:
- Investing in people, even when results take time
- Maintaining standards, even when shortcuts are tempting
- Committing to growth, even when progress is slow

In martial arts, mastery is earned over years of dedicated training. Leadership is no different. Those who chase quick results sacrifice long-term gains. Disciplined leaders know success requires endurance and perseverance.

The Strength of Personal Accountability

Accountability begins with the leader. Before you hold others responsible, you must first hold yourself to the highest standard.

A leader who practices personal accountability:
- Takes responsibility for outcomes—both success and failure
- Seeks feedback and acts on it
- Admits mistakes without defensively
- Commits to continuous improvement

This level of ownership creates trust. When your team observes your accountability, they're more likely to do the same. Accountability is a shared value.

The Cultural Effect of Discipline

Leadership discipline does not remain personal—it becomes cultural.

Over time, your habits shape your team's behavior. Your standards become their standards. Your discipline becomes the organization's identity.

A disciplined leader creates:
- Clarity in communication
- Efficiency in execution

- Trust within the team
- Consistency in performance

Culture is not created with words but with repetition. Every action reinforces the culture you are building.

Communication as a Discipline

Communication is one of the clearest reflections of leadership discipline. Disciplined leaders communicate with:
- Clarity
- Purpose
- Consistency

They do not speak to impress—they speak to guide. They:
- Set clear expectations
- Provide timely feedback
- Pay attention and intentionally.
- Avoid reactive or emotionally driven communication.

Disciplined communication boosts alignment—teams work confidently with clear direction.

Execution: Turning Discipline into Results

Discipline is most visible in execution. Ideas are common. Vision is valuable. But execution is what defines leadership.

Disciplined leaders:
- Break goals into clear, feasible steps
- Monitor progress consistently
- Maintain momentum even when problems emerge.
- Hold themselves and others accountable for results.

Success comes not from bursts, but sustained effort. Execution is not an event—it is a habit.

The Link Between Discipline and Morale

Many leaders overlook the connection between discipline and morale. In reality, disciplined leadership creates settings in which people feel:

- Secure
- Respected
- Valued

When expectations are clear, leaders are consistent, and standards are fairly upheld, teams thrive. High morale comes from security and confidence, not motivation alone.

Disciplined leaders:

- Recognize effort consistently
- Preserve fairness in decision-making.
- Protect the team from unnecessary chaos.
- Model sustainable work habits.

This creates a context in which individuals are not only productive but also engaged and committed.

Building a Culture of Fortitude

One of the greatest outcomes of disciplined leadership is resilience. Organizations led by disciplined individuals tend to be better equipped to handle:

- Change
- Uncertainty
- Adversity

Their foundation is based on principle, not circumstances. Disciplined leaders:

- Maintain values under pressure.
- Adapt without losing direction.
- Respond strategically rather than react emotionally.

Over time, this creates a culture that is hard to shake. A culture that can bend—but not break.

Self-discipline and personal responsibility are essential in leadership.
They define your *credibility*.
They shape your *influence*.
They determine your *legacy*.

As a leader, you are always observed, setting standards, and influencing cultures. The question is not whether you are leading—it is how you are leading.

With discipline, leadership becomes consistent. With accountability, leadership becomes credible. And when both are present, leadership becomes transformational.

CHAPTER 6

Enforcing Discipline with Others: The Leader's Responsibility to Build Standards That Outlast Their Presence

Leadership begins within, but it is proven through others. Many individuals can discipline themselves for a season. Fewer can sustain it. But only true leaders possess the ability to instill discipline in a team, an organization, or a culture that operates effectively even in their absence.

Over the course of my career, whether on the dojang floor training martial artists or in boardrooms consulting executives, I have observed a consistent truth: **the strength of any organization is a direct reflection of the discipline of its leadership—and the discipline that leadership enforces.**

Self-discipline is *personal mastery*.
Enforcing discipline is *leadership mastery*.
There is a *distinct difference*.

Self-discipline requires commitment. Enforcing discipline requires courage, clarity, and consistency.

Many leaders fail at this level—not because they lack intelligence or capability—but because they misunderstand discipline itself.

Discipline is not about *control*.
It is not about *authority*.
It is not about *fear*.
Discipline is about alignment.

Alignment between:
- Standards and behavior
- Values and actions
- Expectations and execution

When alignment is present, performance elevates. When alignment is absent, dysfunction begins. And it is the leader's responsibility—not the team's—to establish and maintain that alignment.

The Leader's Standard: You Cannot Enforce What You Do Not Embody

Before a leader can enforce discipline in others, there is a foundational requirement: **you must first become the standard.**

In martial arts, an instructor cannot demand precision if their own technique is flawed. Students do not follow words, they follow demonstration. The same principle applies in leadership.

You cannot:
- Demand punctuality while arriving late
- Expect accountability while avoiding responsibility
- Require consistency while operating inconsistently

Your behavior sets the tone long before your expectations are communicated. People observe before they comply. In every organization, whether acknowledged or not, there is an unspoken question: *"Is the leader living what they are asking of us?"*

If the answer is *no*, discipline becomes *resistance*.
If the answer is *yes*, discipline becomes *respect*.

Leadership is not enforced through position — it is reinforced through example. When your actions align with your expectations, enforcement becomes natural. Without that alignment, enforcement becomes conflict.

The Art of Setting Standards

A disciplined organization is not built on motivation — it is built on standards. Standards define:
- What is acceptable
- What is expected
- What is non-negotiable

Without standards, leadership becomes subjective. And when leadership becomes subjective, confusion replaces clarity.

In martial arts, there is no ambiguity in a technique. A punch is either correct — or it is not. A stance is either stable — or it is not. This clarity creates excellence. In business and leadership, the same must apply.

A leader must establish standards that are:

1. Clear

There must be no room for interpretation. Vague expectations create inconsistent results. **Do not say**: "Do your best." **Define**: "What does excellence look like in this role?" Clarity removes confusion. Confusion eliminates performance.

2. Relevant:

Standards must connect directly to purpose. If a rule does not serve the mission, it becomes unnecessary resistance. Every standard should answer: "How does this improve performance, culture, or results?" Relevance creates buy-in.

3. Consistent:

Standards must apply equally—without exception. The moment a leader applies discipline selectively, credibility begins to erode. Consistency builds trust. Inconsistency destroys it.

4. Measurable:

If you cannot measure it, you cannot enforce it. Standards must have observable outcomes.

In martial arts:

- ❖ Did the technique land correctly?
- ❖ Was the form executed properly?

In business:

- ❖ Was the deadline met?
- ❖ Was the quality achieved?

Measurement creates accountability.

Boundaries: The Structure of Discipline

Standards define expectations. **Boundaries protect them**. Without boundaries, standards lose their power. Boundaries are not restrictions, they are structures. They create:

- Stability
- Focus
- Predictability

In both martial arts and leadership, structure produces freedom, not limitation. A student who trains within structured discipline gains greater freedom of movement, adaptability, and mastery. Similarly, a team operating within clear boundaries performs with greater confidence and efficiency.

Essential Boundaries Leaders Must Establish:

- Communication Standards: how information is shared, escalated, and addressed
- Time Discipline: punctuality, deadlines, and priorities
- Performance Expectations: Output quality and consistency
- Behavioral Conduct: Respect, professionalism, and interaction

Boundaries eliminate *uncertainty*.
And where there is no uncertainty, there is *no hesitation*.

Consistency: The Foundation of Trust

If I were to identify one principle that separates strong leaders from weak ones, it would be this: **Consistency**.

Consistency is the foundation upon which trust is built. Without it:

- Standards lose credibility
- Teams lose direction
- Culture begins to fracture

A leader who enforces discipline one day and ignores it the next creates instability. And instability leads to:

- Frustration
- Confusion
- Disengagement

Consistency communicates: "These standard matters—every time."

In martial arts, consistency is what builds muscle memory. In leadership, consistency builds cultural memory. It teaches people: "What is expected—always."

Coaching Over Control

One of the greatest misconceptions in leadership is the belief that discipline requires force. It does not. Force creates compliance. **Coaching creates commitment**.

A leader who only corrects behavior without developing understanding creates temporary change—but not lasting growth. True discipline is not about correction—it is about development.

A disciplined leader coaches by:

- Seeking understanding before judgment
- Explaining the "why" behind standards
- Providing clear, actionable feedback

- Equipping individuals with tools for improvement

In martial arts, correction is constant—but it is purposeful. The instructor does not simply say: "You are wrong." They demonstrate: "This is the correct way—and here is how to achieve it." Leadership must operate the same way.

People do not resist discipline; they resist confusion and unfairness. When discipline is explained, modeled, and supported—it becomes embraced.

Accountability: Protecting the Standard

There will come a time in every leader's journey when coaching is not enough.

When standards are *ignored*.
When behavior *does not change*.
When alignment is *broken repeatedly*.

At that point, accountability becomes necessary. And this is where many leaders fail—not because they do not see the issue, but because they avoid the discomfort of addressing it.

Avoidance *weakens* leadership.
Accountability *strengthens* it.
Accountability is not punishment.
It is protection.

Protection of:
- The culture
- The standards
- The individuals who uphold them

Forms of Accountability May Include:
- Direct feedback and correction
- Performance improvement plans
- Adjusted responsibilities
- Increased oversight
- Separation from the organization

A disciplined leader does not hesitate to act when necessary. Because every moment of inaction communicates: **"This behavior is acceptable."** And once that message is sent, standards begin to collapse.

The Balance: Discipline and Compassion

There is a misconception that strong discipline requires harshness. This is incorrect. True leadership balances two forces: **Discipline and compassion**.

Discipline without compassion creates fear.
Compassion without discipline creates weakness.
But when balanced correctly, they create strength.

A leader must:
- Hold high expectations
- Recognize human challenges
- Provide support when needed
- Maintain standards regardless

In martial arts, a master pushes the student—but never abandons them. They demand excellence—but they guide the journey. Leadership must reflect the same balance.

People perform best when they feel:
- Challenged
- Supported
- Respected

Building a Culture of Self-Discipline

The ultimate goal of leadership is not control—it is independence. A truly disciplined organization does not rely on constant supervision. Instead, it operates on:
- Internal accountability
- Shared standards
- Collective responsibility

In such an environment:
- Individuals correct themselves
- Teams hold each other accountable
- Excellence becomes the norm

This is the highest level of leadership. Where discipline is no longer enforced, it is lived.

The Leader's Legacy

Leadership is temporary. Culture is lasting. The question every leader must ask is: **"What remains when I am no longer present?"** If discipline depends solely on your *presence*, your leadership is incomplete. If discipline continues in your *absence*, your leadership has become legacy.

A disciplined leader creates systems, standards, and expectations that endure. They build:
- Strong individuals
- Strong teams
- Strong cultures

And those systems continue long after they step away.

Final Reflection: The True Measure of Leadership

Discipline is not developed through motivation. It is developed through:
- Structure
- Standards
- Consistency
- Accountability

As a leader, your responsibility is clear:
- Define the standard
- Model the behavior
- Enforce expectations
- Protect the culture

Because people do not rise to the level of their intentions. **They rise to the level of the standards they are held to**. And it is the leader—always the leader—who defines that level.

Closing Principle

In both martial arts and leadership, there is a truth that cannot be ignored:

Weak standards create *weak* outcomes.
Strong standards create *strong* people.
And *strong* people build *strong* organizations.

So do not hesitate to lead with discipline. Do not hesitate to enforce standards. Do not hesitate to protect what matters.

Because in the end: **discipline is not what limits people—it is what elevates them.**

CHAPTER 7

Earning Respect vs. Demanding It

In leadership, respect is essential. Respect is the core of influence. Without it, influence fades, authority weakens, and leadership is powerless. One of the most critical distinctions a leader must understand is this: **Respect cannot be demanded—it must be earned**.

Throughout my journey in martial arts and business, I have observed that the most respected leaders are not those who hold the highest titles, but those who consistently demonstrate character, competence, and care for others. True respect is not granted by position—it is given in response to how one leads.

The Illusion of Demanded Respect

Many leaders make the mistake of believing that authority automatically commands respect. They rely on their title, rank, or control to enforce obedience, mistaking compliance for loyalty. This is what I call the *illusion of demanded respect*. Demanded respect relies on hierarchy and controls 'Respect me because I am in charge.' While this approach may produce immediate results, it is both fragile and unsustainable. What appears to be respect is often nothing more than surface-level compliance—people follow instructions but do not follow the leader.

As highlighted in the foundational principles of leadership, demanded respect is not genuine—it is compliance masquerading as respect.

Why Demanded Respect Fails

1. It Relies on Fear, Not Trust

Leadership built on fear may produce obedience, but it will never produce commitment. Fear suppresses communication. It silences feedback. It creates an environment where individuals operate cautiously rather than confidently. In such environments:

- ❖ Innovation declines
- ❖ Initiative disappears
- ❖ Honesty is replaced with avoidance.

A leader may believe they are in control, but in reality, they are leading a disengaged team. Trust, on the other hand, creates strength. It allows individuals to contribute openly, take calculated risks, and operate with confidence. Leaders who cultivate trust unlock potential, those who rely on fear limit it.

2. It Is Conditional and Superficial

Respect that is tied to position is temporary. When respect is demanded, it exists only as long as authority is present. The moment the title is removed, influence disappears. This respect is transactional—it is given out of obligation, not merit. Externally, this may appear as politeness and compliance, but it often hides disengagement and frustration. True respect is rooted in character. It remains even when the leader is no longer presenter in the role.

3. It Suppresses Growth and Innovation

Environments driven by demanded respect are environments where growth is limited. When individuals fear making mistakes or challenging ideas, they stop thinking creatively. They stop contributing fully. They operate within safe boundaries—not because they lack ability, but because they lack psychological safety. Innovation requires freedom. Growth requires the ability to fail, learn, and adapt. Leaders who demand respect often unknowingly create ceilings for their teams. Leaders who earn respect remove those ceilings.

4. It Creates Resistance, Not Loyalty

Demanded respect does not build loyalty, it builds quiet resistance. This resistance is rarely loud. It is subtle:

- ❖ Minimal effort instead of full engagement
- ❖ Silence instead of honest feedback
- ❖ Agreement in public, disagreement in private

Over time, this creates division within the organization—a clear separation between leadership and team members. An "us versus them" culture begins to form. Leadership becomes something people endure—not something they believe in.

The Essence of Earned Respect

Earned respect is entirely different. It is not imposed—it is given. It is built over time through consistent actions that reflect:

- Integrity
- Competence
- Fairness
- Empathy
- Accountability

Leaders who earn respect:
- Lead by example
- Keep their commitments
- Admit their mistakes
- Treat all individuals with dignity.
- Make decisions based on principle, not ego.

This form of respect inspires commitment—not mere compliance. People follow not because they have to, but because they want to.

The Leadership Advantage of Earned Respect

When respect is earned, leadership transforms. A respected leader can:
- Inspire voluntary effort and dedication.
- Navigate conflict with composure and credibility.
- Encourage open communication and honest feedback.
- Lead change with alignment rather than resistance.

Respect is the true foundation of influence.
It *stabilizes* teams during *uncertainty*.
It *strengthens* relationships during *adversity*.
It *builds* unity where *division* might otherwise exist.

Barriers to Earning Respect

Leaders often lose respect not through major failures, but through consistent misalignment. Respect is eroded when leaders:

- Act inconsistently
- Fail to follow through on commitments.
- Prioritize ego over team success.
- Avoid accountability
- Expect standards that they do not uphold.

These behaviors create doubt, weaken credibility, and diminish influence. A title cannot compensate for a lack of integrity.

How Leaders Earn Respect

Respect is earned through daily actions, not occasional efforts. A disciplined leader must:

- **Demonstrate consistency**–Align words with actions.
- **Listen actively**–Value input from others.
- **Show humility**–Acknowledge limitations and mistakes.
- **Uphold standards**–Lead by the same expectations given to others.
- **Practice fairness**–Treat all individuals with equal respect.
- **Lead with purpose**–Focus on mission, not personal validation.

Each of these actions reinforces trust. Over time, trust becomes respect—and respect becomes influence.

A Better Way Forward

To lead effectively, one must shift from control to influence. This requires a change in mindset:
- From authority to example
- From dominance to service
- From expectation to accountability

Leadership is not about being followed because you must be—it is about being followed because you should be.

The Legacy of Respect

Respect that is earned does not fade—it endures. Long after titles are gone, positions change, and roles evolve, the impact of a respected leader remains. It lives in the people they developed, the culture they shaped, and the standards they upheld.

Leaders who demand respect may be obeyed in the moment—but often forgotten. Leaders who earn respect are remembered—and, more importantly, replicated. *Their influence becomes a legacy.*

Respect is the foundation of leadership. It cannot be forced, claimed, or sustained by authority alone. It cannot be claimed. It cannot be sustained through authority alone. It must be earned—through consistency, integrity, and service.

Leadership is not about the number who follows you when you have authority—it is defined by how many choose to follow you when they no longer have to.

CHAPTER 8

Respect as the Invisible Architecture of Leadership

Respect is often spoken of as a value. It is placed on walls, printed in mission statements, and referenced in leadership discussions. Yet in my decades of training martial artists, coaching executives, and building organizations, I have come to understand a deeper truth: **Respect is not a statement—it is a structure**.

It is the invisible architecture that holds an organization together when pressure is applied. It is what determines whether a team fractures under adversity or unites in discipline and purpose.

In martial arts, we do not begin with technique—we begin with respect. The bow is not symbolic. It is foundational. It is the first lesson and the last lesson. It is the acknowledgment that growth requires humility, discipline requires structure, and mastery requires honor. The same principle applies in leadership.

An organization without respect may still function—but it will never reach its highest level of performance. An organization grounded in respect, however, becomes something far greater than the sum of its parts. It becomes disciplined, aligned, and resilient.

Respect must evolve from an individual behavior into a collective culture. In this expanded exploration, we will go deeper—into the mechanics, mindset, and mastery required to build, sustain, and protect a culture of mutual respect at the highest level.

The Philosophy of Respect in Leadership

Respect is not passive. It is not soft. It is not optional. **Respect is discipline in action**.

Many leaders misunderstand respect as something that is "earned" only after achievement or position. This belief creates a dangerous hierarchy where respect is conditional rather than foundational.

In martial arts, we do not wait for a student to become a black belt before we respect them. We respect them the moment they step onto the mat—because they have chosen the path of growth. Leadership must operate the same way.

Respect is not a *reward*.
It is a *requirement*.

When respect is conditional:
- Trust becomes unstable
- Communication becomes guarded

- Performance becomes inconsistent

When respect is foundational:
- Trust becomes automatic
- Communication becomes open
- Performance becomes elevated

The warrior-leader understands this distinction.
You do not build *respect* based on *outcomes*.
You build *outcomes* based on *respect*.

Respect Across Hierarchies—Eliminating the Illusion of Rank-Based Value

One of the most significant failures I have observed in both martial arts organizations and corporate environments is the misuse of hierarchy. Hierarchy is necessary for structure. But it must never determine value. This principle is not philosophical, it is operational.

The Danger of Rank-Based Respect

When respect is tied only to rank:
- Leaders become disconnected
- Team members become disengaged
- Innovation becomes suppressed

This creates what I call a "vertical culture"—a system where communication flows upward with hesitation and downward with authority.

In contrast, a culture of mutual respect creates a "circular culture"—where:

- Ideas flow freely
- Contributions are valued equally
- Leadership is reinforced through connection, not control

Martial Arts Application

In the dojang, a beginner bows to a black belt—but the black belt bows back. Why? Because respect is not about superiority, it is about shared commitment to growth. This simple act eliminates ego and reinforces unity.

Business Application

In high-performing organizations:
- Executives listen to entry-level employees
- Managers seek input from their teams
- Leaders recognize contributions regardless of visibility

This does not weaken authority. It strengthens influence. Because when people feel respected, they do not resist leadership, they support it.

Respect in Communication—The Language of Leadership

Communication is where respect becomes visible. You can measure the level of respect in any organization by observing how people speak to one another, especially under pressure.

Three Levels of Communication

Level 1: Transactional Communication: Focused on tasks, often lacking connection

Level 2: Directive Communication: Focused on authority, often lacking collaboration

Level 3: Respect-Based Communication: Focused on clarity, alignment, and mutual understanding The third level is where leadership operates at its highest level.

Principles of Respect-Based Communication

A disciplined leader communicates with:
- **Clarity**–eliminating confusion
- **Control**–eliminating emotional volatility
- **Consideration**–eliminating unnecessary friction

This does not mean avoiding directness. It means delivering directness with discipline.

The Warrior-Leader Standard

Speak to others in a way that:
- Builds them without weakening the standard
- Corrects them without diminishing their value
- Challenges them without creating resistance

This is not easy. It requires mastery of self before mastery of others.

Respect in Conflict—Turning Friction into Strength

Conflict is inevitable. But conflict, when handled correctly, is not destructive, it is developmental. Respectful conflict transforms division into alignment.

The Two Failures in Conflict

Failure 1: Avoidance – problems are ignored
Failure 2: Domination – problems are forced into submission

Both approaches weaken the organization.

The Disciplined Approach to Conflict

The warrior-leader approaches conflict with:
- Composure under pressure
- Focus on solutions, not ego
- Commitment to alignment, not victory

The Martial Arts Parallel

In sparring, the goal is not to destroy your opponent—it is to sharpen your skill. Conflict in leadership must operate the same way.

You are not fighting the *person*.
You are refining the *process*.

Practical Application

When conflict arises:
- Address the issue immediately
- Separate the behavior from the individual
- Always maintain professionalism
- Seek resolution, not dominance

This transforms conflict into a tool for growth.

Respect in Feedback—The Engine of Improvement

Feedback is one of the most powerful tools in leadership. But without respect, it becomes ineffective. Disrespectful feedback creates *resistance*. Respectful feedback creates *growth*.

The Structure of Effective Feedback

A disciplined leader delivers feedback that is:
- Specific–clear and actionable
- Constructive–focused on improvement
- Balanced–recognizing strengths and addressing weaknesses

The Emotional Component

Feedback must be removed:
- Sarcasm
- Frustration
- Ego

And replace them with:
- Purpose
- Clarity
- Direction

Leadership Responsibility

Do not ask: "Did I say what needed to be said?"
Ask: "Was it received in a way that creates improvement?"

Because leadership is not measured by what you say—it is measured by what changes.

Diversity, Inclusion, and the Strength of Perspective

Respect is not complete without inclusion. A respectful culture does not simply tolerate differences—it leverages them. Diversity is not a complication—it is an advantage.

The Leadership Shift

Average leaders seek agreement. Great leaders seek perspective. Why? Because innovation does not come from similarity, it comes from contrast.

The Warrior-Leader Mindset

In martial arts, no two fighters are identical. Different styles, strengths, and strategies create adaptability. The same applies in leadership.

A team that thinks differently—but aligns in values—will outperform a team that thinks the same but lacks perspective.

Building an Inclusive Culture

Leaders must:
- Encourage diverse input
- Eliminate bias through awareness
- Create systems that support participation

Inclusion is not an *initiative*.
It is *discipline*.

Psychological Safety—The Environment Where Excellence Thrives

One of the most critical outcomes of respect is psychological safety.

Without psychological safety, talent is suppressed.
With it, potential is realized.

What psychological safety creates:
- Open communication
- Confident decision-making
- Willingness to take calculated risks
- Accountability without fear

What happens without it:
- Silence replaces contribution
- Fear replaces innovation
- Compliance replaces commitment

The Leader's Role

You do not *demand* psychological safety.
You *create* it through behavior.
Every interaction either *strengthens or weakens it*.

Building a Respect-Based Culture—The Leadership Blueprint

A culture of respect does not happen by accident. It is built intentionally.

1. **Model the Standard**
    Leadership behavior sets the tone.

If you lose composure, others will follow.

If you demonstrate respect, others will reflect on it.

2. Reinforce the Behavior

Recognize and reward:

- ❖ Collaboration
- ❖ Professionalism
- ❖ Accountability

What is reinforced becomes repeated.

3. Create Feedback Systems

Respect must be measured through experience, not assumption. Ask:

- ❖ Do people feel heard?
- ❖ Do they feel valued?
- ❖ Do they feel safe contributing?

4. Address Disrespect Immediately

Tolerance of disrespect is the fastest way to destroy culture. Correction must be:

- ❖ Immediate
- ❖ Consistent
- ❖ Uncompromising

5. Embed Respect into Structure

Respect must be integrated into:

- ❖ Hiring practices
- ❖ Training programs
- ❖ Performance evaluations
- ❖ Leadership development

It must move from philosophy to system.

Sustaining Respect Under Pressure

It is easy to demonstrate respect when conditions are ideal.
The true test of leadership is maintaining respect when:
- Deadlines are tight
- Emotions are high
- Outcomes are uncertain

The Warrior-Leader Principle

Pressure does not create character—it reveals it.
If respect disappears under pressure, it was never embedded—it was conditional.

Discipline Under Stress

Leaders must train themselves to:
- Remain composed
- Communicate clearly
- Lead consistently

This is not *talent*.
It is *training*.

The Legacy of Respect

In the end, leadership is not measured solely by results. It is measured by:
- The environment you create
- The people you develop
- The standard you leave behind

Respect becomes a force multiplier when embedded into culture.

The Long-Term Impact

A respectful culture:
- Retaining talent
- Attracts excellence
- Sustains performance
- Builds legacy

People may forget strategies. They will never forget how they were treated.

Final Reflection: The Warrior-Leader Standard

Respect is not a tactic. It is not a technique. It is the foundation upon which all leadership is built.

The warrior-leader understands:
- Confidence allows you to act
- Discipline allows you to execute
- Respect allows you to lead

Without respect, leadership becomes control. *With respect*, leadership becomes influence. And influence—when grounded in character—becomes legacy.

So, I leave you with this:
Do not ask how to gain more authority.
Ask how to demonstrate more respect.
Because when respect becomes your standard,
Leadership is no longer something you pursue—
It is something you embody.

CHAPTER 9

The Discipline of Daily Execution: Mastering the Unseen Routines That Separate Intention from Achievement

There is a line—thin, invisible, and often ignored—that separates those who achieve from those who merely intend. *It is the invisible line between dreamers and doers.* Talent alone does not make the difference. It is not an opportunity.

Even intelligence is not what sets achievers apart.
Execution makes all the difference.

In my decades as a martial artist and business leader, I have encountered countless individuals with extraordinary vision. They speak of greatness. They declare their goals with passion. They attend seminars, read books, and surround themselves with inspiration. Yet, most never arrive at the destination they so vividly describe. *Why?*

Because intention without execution is an illusion. The warrior-leader understands a fundamental truth: **success is not built in moments of inspiration; it is forged in moments of repetition.**

Daily execution is the bridge between who you are and who you are called to become. It is not glamorous. It is not always visible. But it is always decisive.

In martial arts, we do not rise to the level of our expectations—we fall to the level of our training. In business, the same principle applies. You do not perform based on what you hope to do; you perform based on what you consistently do.

Commit to mastering consistency, this is your greatest daily leverage for achievement.

The Myth of Motivation

One of the greatest misconceptions in leadership and personal development is the belief that motivation is the driving force behind success.

Motivation is *temporary*.
Discipline is *permanent*.

Motivation arrives when conditions are favorable—when energy is high, when circumstances align, when the environment is supportive. But what happens when:
- Are you tired?
- Are you discouraged?
- Are you uncertain?

This is where most *people stop*.
This is where the *warrior continues*.

In martial arts training, we do not ask, "Do I feel like training today?" We ask, "What must be done today to honor my commitment?" That is discipline. Discipline transforms emotion into action and sets a consistent standard, regardless of mood.

Lead with consistency; your team's execution depends on your reliability.

The Power of the Daily Standard

Execution begins with a standard.
Not a goal.
Not a vision.
A standard.
A goal is something you aim for.
A standard is something you live by.

In the dojang, every student learns the importance of daily fundamentals:
- Proper stance
- Controlled breathing
- Precision in movement
- Respect in conduct

These are not optional practices. They require disciplines.
In business, the same applies. High-performing leaders establish non-negotiable daily standards such as:
- Showing up prepared
- Communicating clearly

- Following through on commitments
- Prioritizing high-impact actions

***KEY TAKEAWAY**: maintain daily standards—consistency outperforms complexity every time. The warrior-leader does not negotiate with their standard. They embody it.

The Discipline of Structure

Execution without structure leads to inconsistency.
Structure creates rhythm.
Rhythm creates momentum.
Momentum creates results.

In martial arts, every training session follows a structure:
1. Warm-up
2. Fundamentals
3. Technique refinement
4. Application (sparring or drills)
5. Reflection

This structure is not random—it is intentional. It ensures that every session contributes to growth.

In business and leadership, your day must also be structured with intention. A disciplined day often includes:
- **Morning Alignment**: Reviewing goals, priorities, and mindset
- **Focused Work Blocks**: Executing high-value tasks without distraction
- **Communication Windows**: Managing emails, calls, and team interactions
- **Skill Development**: Continuous learning and improvement

- **Evening Reflection**: Evaluating performance and identifying adjustments

Without structure, you become reactive. Strategic structure directs your day—this is the foundation for effective execution. The warrior-leader does not drift through the day—they direct it.

The Unseen Work

There is a reality that many do not want to accept: the majority of success is built in moments no one sees.

The early mornings.
The late nights.
The repetition of fundamentals.
The quiet refinement of skill.

In martial arts, a black belt is not earned in front of an audience. It is earned in thousands of unseen repetitions.
In business, the same truth applies. The presentations, the recognition, the awards, these are visible outcomes. But they are the result of invisible discipline.

Take pride in the unseen work; this hidden discipline is the ultimate key to achievement. They understand that:
- Every repetition strengthens identity.
- Every small action compound over time
- Every disciplined choice builds credibility.

You cannot skip the unseen and expect the seen to manifest.

Eliminating Decision Fatigue

One of the hidden enemies of execution is decision fatigue. Every day, individuals make hundreds of decisions. What to do, when to do it, how to do it. Each decision consumes energy. The disciplined leader eliminates unnecessary decisions through routine.

In martial arts, we do not decide how to bow, stand, or execute a basic technique each time. These are ingrained through repetition. In leadership, you must do the same.

Create routines for:
- Morning preparation
- Task prioritization
- Communication processes
- Health and fitness
- Learning and development

When routines are established, execution becomes automatic. Reduce decision-automate routines so execution becomes effortless and focused.

The Role of Accountability

Discipline thrives in accountability. In the dojang, students are accountable to:
- Their instructor
- Their peers
- The standard of the art

This accountability creates a culture of excellence.

In business, leaders must establish systems of accountability that reinforce execution. This includes:

- Clear expectations
- Measurable outcomes
- Regular check-ins
- Honest feedback

But the most important level of accountability is self-accountability. The warrior-leaders hold themselves to a higher standard than anyone else. They do not wait to be corrected. They correct themselves.

The Compounding Effect of Consistency

Small actions, repeated daily, create extraordinary results. This is the law of compounding.

In martial arts:

- One punch practiced 10,000 times becomes instinctive.
- One stance refined daily becomes unshakable.
- One principle applied consistently becomes mastery.

In business:

- One call per day becomes 365 opportunities per year.
- One improvement per week transforms an organization.
- One disciplined habit reshapes a career.

The problem is *not* that people *do not take action*.
The problem is that they *do not sustain action*.

Consistency turns effort into identity. When execution becomes who you are—not just what you do—success becomes inevitable.

Overcoming Resistance

Every day, resistance will appear. It may come in the form of:
- Procrastination
- Doubt
- Distraction
- Fatigue

Resistance is not a sign to *stop*.
It is a signal to *execute*.

In martial arts training, discomfort is expected. Fatigue is normal. Difficulty is part of the process. The warrior does not avoid resistance—they train through it. In leadership, you must adopt the same mindset.

When resistance appears, ask:
- What is the next action?
- What is the smallest step forward?
- What must be done regardless of how I feel?

Execution is not about eliminating resistance. It is about moving forward despite it.

Precision Over Perfection

Perfection is the enemy of execution. Many individuals delay action because they are waiting for the perfect plan, the perfect timing, or the perfect conditions. The warrior-leader does not wait for perfection. They pursue precision.

Precision means:
- Taking action with clarity
- Learning from feedback
- Adjusting with intention

In martial arts, a technique is not perfected in theory, it is refined through practice. In business, the same principle applies.

Execution creates *feedback*.
Feedback creates *improvement*.
Improvement creates *excellence*.
You cannot improve what you do not execute.

Building Identity Through Execution

At the highest level, discipline is not about tasks, it is about identity. You are not someone who occasionally executes. You are an executor.

In martial arts, a black belt is not defined by a certificate. They are defined by their habits, their mindset, and their consistency.

In leadership, your identity is shaped by your daily actions. Every day, you are casting votes for the person you are becoming.
- When you follow through, you become reliable.
- When you show up prepared, you become professional.
- When you execute consistently, you become a leader.

Identity is not *declared*.
It is *demonstrated*.

The Warrior-Leader's Daily Code

To master daily execution, the warrior-leader lives by a code:

1. I execute regardless of how I feel.
2. I prioritize what matters most.
3. I honor my commitments.
4. I refine my craft daily.
5. I embrace discipline as freedom.

This code is not *recited*—it is *lived*.

The Path of Daily Mastery

The discipline of daily execution is not a one-time decision. It is a daily commitment. It is choosing, again and again, to act with purpose, to follow through, and to honor your standard.

In martial arts, mastery is not achieved in a single moment. It is the result of years of disciplined practice. In leadership, the same truth applies.

The warrior-leader does not seek shortcuts. They seek consistency. They understand that greatness is not an event, it is a process. And that process is built one day at a time.

Final Reflection

Ask yourself:

- What are my daily standards?
- Where am I inconsistent?
- What will I execute today, no matter what?

Do not wait for the perfect moment.
The moment is *now*.
Execute!

CHAPTER 10

Resilience—The Warrior's Response to Failure: Transforming Setbacks into Strategic Advantages Through Mental Conditioning

Failure is not the opposite of success—it is the forge in which success is created.

In over four decades of training martial artists and consulting business leaders, I have witnessed a consistent truth: **those who rise are not those who avoid failure, but those who develop a disciplined relationship with it**.

The untrained mind sees *failure as defeat*.
The conditioned mind sees *failure as data*.
The warrior-leader sees *failure as direction*.

Resilience is a discipline to develop, not inherit. It means absorbing impact and returning with clarity, a stronger strategy, and conviction.

In martial arts, we train to respond after being struck, not simply to avoid it. Likewise, leaders will face rejection, make mistakes, and encounter setbacks.

The question is not whether you will fail.
The question is: **How will you respond when you do**?

Redefining Failure—From Emotional Reaction to Strategic Feedback

Most individual's experience failure emotionally before they experience it intellectually. This is where the breakdown begins. They internalize failure:

- "I am not good enough."
- "This is not working."
- "Maybe I am not meant for this."

This mindset is not only inaccurate, it is dangerous. Failure is not a reflection of your identity. Failure is a reflection of your current method.

As martial artists, when a technique fails, we do not abandon the art—we refine its execution. When a strike misses, we do not question our worth—we adjust our timing. The same principle applies in business and leadership.

A failed product launch is not a verdict on your capability— it is feedback on your strategy. A failed conversation is not a sign of weakness—it is an opportunity to refine communication. A failed decision is not the end—it is the beginning of clarity.

The warrior-leader separates **self** from **strategy**. This separation is critical. Without it, failure becomes personal.

When failure becomes personal, resilience becomes impossible.

To develop resilience, you must adopt a disciplined reframing process:

1. **Detach Emotion from Outcome:**
Feel the impact, but do not let it define your perception.

2. **Extract the Lesson Immediately:**
Ask: *What specifically did this experience teach me?*

3. **Apply the Adjustment Without Delay**
Speed of correction is the foundation of resilience.

***KEY TAKEAWAY**: Failure, when understood correctly, becomes wisdom you can apply immediately.

The Martial Arts Mindset—Conditioning the Response

In the dojang, we train *response*, not *reaction*.
Reaction is emotional, impulsive, and uncontrolled.
Response is disciplined, intentional, and trained.

***KEY TAKEAWAY**: Resilience is built by training intentional responses, not by relying on reactions.

A reactive individual:
- Avoids challenges after failure
- Hesitates in decision-making
- Seeks comfort instead of growth

A responsive warrior-leader:
- Moves toward challenge
- Refining decision-making through experience
- Seeks growth through discomfort

Mental conditioning is the bridge between failure and resilience. In martial arts, conditioning is repetitive. We drill movements thousands of times until they become instinctive.

The same must be done with the mindset. You must train your mental response to failure with the same discipline you train your physical technique.

Mental Conditioning Practices for Resilience

- **Visualization Training**: see yourself encountering setbacks—and overcoming them. Condition your mind to expect resistance.
- **Controlled Adversity Exposure**: intentionally place yourself in challenging situations. Growth requires friction.
- **Reflection Protocols**: after every failure, document
  - What happened
  - What was within your control
  - What will be done differently next time?
- **Identity Reinforcement**: Emphasize: *"I am defined by response, not outcomes."*

***KEY TAKEAWAY**: The more you practice recovery routines, the stronger your automatic resilience becomes.

Emotional Mastery—Stability Under Pressure

Resilience is not the absence of emotion. It is the mastery of it. In both combat and leadership, emotional instability leads to poor decisions.

When a fighter becomes frustrated, they lose technique. When a leader becomes overwhelmed, they lose clarity. Failure often triggers:

- Frustration
- Self-doubt
- Fear of repetition

If left unmanaged, these emotions compound the original setback. The warrior-leader develops emotional discipline through awareness and control.

Three Levels of Emotional Mastery

Level 1: Recognition: Identify the emotion without judgment. *"I am experiencing frustration."*

Level 2: Regulation: Control your physiological state:

- Breathing techniques
- Posture alignment
- Strategic pauses

Level 3: Redirection: Channel the energy into productive action. Emotion is energy. When directed, it becomes fuel. When uncontrolled, it becomes interference.

In my experience, the most dangerous moment is not failure itself, it is the emotional reaction that follows it.

***KEY TAKEAWAY**: Master your emotional response to failure to control your future direction.

The Discipline of Recovery—Returning Stronger

In martial arts, after impact comes recovery.
You are *knocked down*.
You *regain your stance*.
You *re-engage*.
This is *resilience in action*.

Recovery is not passive. It is a disciplined process. Many individuals fail not because of the initial setback, but because they delay their return. They remain in analysis, hesitation, or self-pity. The warrior-leader returns quickly—but intelligently.

The Recovery Framework:

1. **Stabilize:** Regain composure. Do not act from emotional volatility.
2. **Assess:** What specifically caused the breakdown?
3. **Adjust:** Modify strategy, not identity.
4. **Re-engage:** Take action immediately. Momentum must be restored.

Speed matters. The longer you stay down, the more doubt accumulates.

In business, I have seen organizations recover from major losses—not because they avoided mistakes, but because they moved decisively after them.

In martial arts, the fighter who recovers fastest often wins—even after being struck. Resilience is not measured by how hard you fall.

***KEY TAKEAWAY**: True resilience is measured by your ability to rise after setbacks.

Strategic Adaptation—Turning Setbacks into Advantage

Failure provides information that your success cannot. When everything is working, you learn very little. When things break down, the system reveals itself. The warrior-leader uses failure as a strategic advantage.

Key Questions for Strategic Adaptation:

- What assumption proved incorrect?
- Where was my preparation insufficient?
- What variable did I overlook?
- What pattern is emerging?

This level of analysis transforms failure into insight. In business, market failures reveal customer behavior. In leadership, communication failures reveal team dynamics. In martial arts, technical failures reveal gaps in skill. Every setback contains a blueprint for improvement.

***KEY TAKEAWAY**: Only disciplined analysis turns failures into strategic advantages.

Strategic adaptation requires humility—the willingness to acknowledge that your previous approach was incomplete.

This is not a *weakness*.
This is *mastery*.

Building Resilience Through Repetition

Resilience is not developed in a single moment. It is built through repeated challenges. Just as muscles grow through resistance, resilience grows through adversity. The key is not to seek failure—but to engage fully in challenges where failure is possible.

Avoidance *weakens* resilience.
Engagement *strengthens* it.

In my training, I emphasize progressive difficulty:
- Start with manageable challenges.
- Increase complexity over time.
- Maintain consistent exposure to discomfort.

This builds confidence—not because you succeed every time, but because you learn you can handle setbacks. Confidence rooted in success is fragile.

***KEY TAKEAWAY**: Build confidence in resilience, not just in success.

Leadership Through Resilience—Setting the Standard

As a leader, your response to failure does not affect only you, it affects everyone around you.

Your team watches:
- How you handle pressure
- How you respond to mistakes
- How quickly you recover

If you react *emotionally*, they become *uncertain*.
If you *withdraw*, they *lose confidence* in you.
If you respond with *discipline*, they become *stronger*.
Leadership is *modeling*.

The warrior-leader demonstrates resilience through:
- Composure under pressure
- Clarity after setbacks
- Decisive action moving forward

When your team sees this consistently, resilience becomes part of the culture. They begin to understand:
- Failure is not punished, it is analyzed.
- Mistakes are not hidden; they are corrected.
- Challenges are not avoided, they are embraced.

*KEY TAKEAWAY: A resilient leader fosters growth, innovation, and trust in the team.

The Identity of the Resilient Warrior

At the highest level, resilience is not something you do but who you become.

You no longer *fear failure.*
You no longer *avoid risk.*
You no longer *hesitate after setbacks.*

You operate with the understanding that:
- Every challenge strengthens you.
- Every setback teaches you.
- Every failure refines you.

This identity shift is critical. When resilience is part of your identity, your behavior aligns with it.

You do not need *motivation.*
You do not need *reassurance.*
You move forward because that is who you are.

Failure is *inevitable.* Defeat is *optional.* The warrior-leader does not measure success by the absence of setbacks, but by the strength of response.

You will be *tested.*
You will be *challenged.*
You will experience moments where *progress seems to stop.*

***KEY TAKEAWAY**: Your response to adversity—not the event—defines your personal and professional identity.

Stand up.
Refocus.
Re-engage.
Transform every setback into a strategy.
Transform every failure into fuel.

Transform every challenge into growth.
This is resilience.
This is leadership.
This is the way of the warrior.

CHAPTER 11

Legacy Leadership—Leading Beyond Your Lifetime

In martial arts, mastery is measured by how enduring your teachings are long after you've gone. In business, we do not measure success solely by revenue, but by whether the organization can thrive without its founder.

Great leadership is measured by continuity, not control. Legacy leadership is the final evolution of the warrior-leader. Transitioning to legacy leadership means shifting from acting alone to creating enduring impact through others. It is moving from individual presence to building lasting systems.

After decades in martial arts training, business leadership, and organizational development, I have come to understand this truth: **if everything depends on you, you have built a system of dependency—not a legacy.** Legacy leadership builds something effective *because* of you, not *dependent* on you.

It is the intentional act of designing systems, cultivating people, and instilling principles that will outlive your physical presence.

This is not *an accident*.
This is not something you *"get to later."*
This is the responsibility of *every serious leader*.

The Shift from Leader to Legacy Builder

There comes a moment in every leader's journey when the question changes. Early in your career, the questions are:
- *How do I succeed?*
- *How do I grow?*
- *How do I lead?*

But at the highest level, the question becomes: *What remains when I am no longer here?* This is where most leaders fall short. They build strong businesses but weak succession plans. They develop personal brands but fail to transfer knowledge. They create success but not sustainability.

In martial arts, I have seen schools close within months of a master stepping away—not because the art was weak, but because the structure was.

In business, I have seen companies collapse after a founder retires—not because the market disappeared, but because there was no leadership pipeline.

To build a legacy, shift focus from being the central figure to establishing a strong system that endures beyond you.

The Three Pillars of Legacy Leadership

Legacy is not built on intention—it is built on structure. There are three foundational pillars every legacy leader must establish:

Pillar 1: Systems — The Structure That Sustains

A system is what allows consistency without constant supervision.

In martial arts, systems include:
- Curriculum progression (belt systems)
- Training protocols
- Testing standards
- Teaching methodologies

In business, systems include:
- Operational processes
- Sales frameworks
- Customer experience models
- Financial management structures

Without systems in place, organizations rely solely on the individual characteristics and direct involvement of certain people, making outcomes unpredictable and heavily influenced by personalities. And personality-driven organizations are fragile.

A true legacy leader asks:
- Can this operate without me?
- Is this documented?
- Is this repeatable?

If the answer is no, you are not building a legacy. You are building reliance.

Pillar 2: People—The Carriers of the Vision

Systems alone are insufficient. People need to execute systems. In martial arts, we do not just train fighters, we train instructors. In business, we do not just hire employees, we develop leaders.

Legacy leadership requires:
- Mentorship
- Leadership development
- Responsibility delegation
- Character cultivation

Your role is not to create followers. Your role is to create future leaders who think, decide, and lead independently.

Ask yourself:
- Who can replace me?
- Who can improve what I started?
- Who understands not just what we do—but why do we do it?

If you cannot answer those questions clearly, your legacy is at risk.

Pillar 3: Principles—The Foundation That Guides

Systems can be copied. People can change. But principles—when deeply instilled—endure.

In martial arts, principles include:
- Discipline

- Respect
- Integrity
- Perseverance

In business, principles include:
- Ethical decision-making
- Accountability
- Service-driven leadership
- Long-term thinking

Principles guide behavior when no one is watching. They ensure that, even in your absence, decisions align with your vision.

Legacy leadership shapes how people think and act when you are not present, not by controlling specifics but by instilling foundational thinking.

The Danger of Leader Dependency

One of the greatest threats to legacy is dependency on the leader. This often looks like:
- Every decision must go through you.
- No one feels empowered to act independently.
- Knowledge is centralized—not shared.
- Growth stalls without your direct involvement

This creates a bottleneck, where progress slows because everything must pass through a single person, much like traffic at a narrow road. And eventually, it creates burnout.

I have worked with martial arts school owners who could not take a vacation without their business declining. I have consulted with business leaders who were afraid to step away because *"everything falls apart without me."*

This is not *leadership*.
This is *entrapment*.

A legacy leader understands: **If your presence is required for survival, your leadership has not matured.**

Building a Leadership Pipeline

Legacy is not built at the end of your career—it is built throughout it. You must continuously identify, develop, and empower future leaders.

Step 1: Identify Potential

Look beyond skill. Instead, look for:
- Character
- Consistency
- Commitment
- Coachability

In martial arts, the best black belts are not always the most talented—they are the most disciplined. In business, the best leaders are not always the most charismatic—they are the most reliable.

Step 2: Develop Through Responsibility

Leadership is not taught—it is developed through experience. Give your future leaders:
- Real responsibilities

- Decision-making authority
- Opportunities to lead under pressure

Then guide them—not by controlling them, but by coaching them.

Step 3: Transfer Ownership

At some point, you must let go. This is where many leaders struggle.

They *hold on* too long.
They *micromanage*.
They *do not trust* those they trained.

Building legacy means trusting and empowering others to take meaningful ownership. It takes courage to step back and let others step forward.

Documenting Vision

If your knowledge is only in your head, it will leave with you. Legacy leaders document everything. This includes:
- Training manuals
- Operational systems
- Leadership philosophies
- Core values
- Strategic frameworks

In martial arts, when knowledge and methods are written down and systematically passed on, that is how styles and traditions endure through many generations, much like a story preserved throughout time. In business, this is how companies scale and sustain.

Documentation creates *clarity*.
Clarity creates *consistency*.
Consistency creates *continuity*.

The Invisible Legacy

Systems are visible.
People are visible.

Culture works in an organization in ways that are often unseen—it cannot be easily measured as systems can, nor is it as obvious as the people involved, but it often has a more significant impact, similar to how the wind shapes a landscape, even though you cannot see the wind itself.

Culture is:
- How people treat each other
- How decisions are made
- What is tolerated
- What is expected

As a leader, you are constantly shaping culture—whether you realize it or not. Legacy leadership requires intentional culture design. Ask yourself:
- What behaviors do we reward?
- What standards do we enforce?
- What attitudes do we tolerate?

Because over time, culture becomes self-sustaining. And that culture will define your legacy long after you are gone.

The Courage to Step Aside

One of the greatest tests of leadership is knowing when to step aside. This does not mean abandoning your role. It means transitioning your role from:

- Leader → Advisor
- Operator → Strategist
- Instructor → Mentor

In martial arts, a true master does not hold the spotlight forever. They elevate their students. They allow the next generation to lead.

In business, the same principle applies. If you do not create space for others to rise, you limit your organization's future.

Legacy vs. Ego

Let me speak directly. Many leaders do not build a legacy because of ego.

They want to be *needed*.
They want to be *the center*.
They want recognition *tied to their presence*.

True legacy requires humility and an honest assessment: Are you creating lasting value or just cementing your role? It requires you to ask:

- Am I building something bigger than myself?
- Or am I building something that revolves around me?

A true legacy leader is not concerned with credit. They are concerned with continuity.

Measuring Legacy

How do you know if you have built a legacy?

Not by *titles*.
Not by *awards*.
Not by *recognition*.

You measure legacy by:
- What continues without you
- Who rises because of you?
- What impact remains beyond you

In martial arts:
- Do your students teach others?
- Do your principles live on in their instruction?

In business:
- Does your organization thrive without your daily involvement?
- Are your systems still producing results?

Legacy is defined not by what you leave behind, but by what continues after you. Legacy is what continues forward.

The Warrior-Leader's Final Responsibility

As a warrior-leader, your final responsibility is not to lead forever. It is to ensure leadership continues.

You are not here to be *permanent*.
You are here to be *impactful*.

And the highest level of impact is not what you achieve—but what you enable others to achieve.

Final Reflection: Beyond Your Lifetime

There is a saying in martial arts: *A true master plants trees—not for their own immediate benefit, but so others may enjoy the shade in the future, even if the master never personally does.*

That is legacy.

It is the discipline to build for a future you may not personally experience. It is the vision to see beyond your own timeline. It is the commitment to ensure that what you started does not end with you.

Closing Words

In my journey as a martial artist, business leader, and mentor, I have come to understand this:

Leadership is *temporary*.
Legacy is *permanent*.

You *will not* always be present.
You *will not* always lead the class.
You *will not* always make the decisions.

But what you *build*—
The systems you *create*—
The people you *develop*—
The principles you *instill*—
Those can endure for generations.

So, I leave you with this final challenge:
Do not just lead for *today*.
Build for *tomorrow*.
And create something that lives *beyond your lifetime*.

That is the path of the true warrior-leader.

ABOUT THE AUTHOR

Grandmaster Stephen Miller was born and raised in Northfield, NJ, and currently lives in Mays Landing, NJ, with his wife, Robin, and their dog Dakota. On his 16th birthday, his parents gifted him his first lessons at the local Taekwondo school. Forty-two years later, he continues to train and teach.

Accomplishments:
- Holds a seventh-degree black belt from the United States National Taekwondo Federation.
- Holds a sixth-degree black belt from the Kukkiwon, in South Korea, and had the honor of testing there in 2019.
- Holds a first-degree black belt in the art of Koyro Gumdo (Korean swords), from the World Koryo Gumdo Association. He is the only black belt in this art in the state of New Jersey.
- 2012: International Champion in Poomse
- 2023: Inducted into the Masters of Martial Arts Hall of Fame.
- 2024: Inducted into both the Action Martial Arts Magazine and the American Martial Arts Alliance Hall of Honor
- 2025: Inducted into the United States Martial Arts Hall of Fame and became a member of the Hongik E-hwa Master's training group.

- Trained in South Korea on three occasions: 1988, 2008, and 2019 and is returning there July 2026 to further his knowledge.
- Won the Gold Medal as the Best Martial Arts Studio in the Best of the Press contest 2023, 2024, and 2025
- Featured co-author in the best-selling *Elite Martial Artists Series, Vol III & IV*

stephenmillerauthor.com